A Prayer with a Purpose

Ivan E Street, MBE

MOORLEY'S Print & Publishing

British Library Cataloguing in Publication Data.
A catalogue record for this book is available from the British Library.

ISBN 978 086071 609 9

MOORLEY'S Print & Publishing
23 Park Rd., Ilkeston, Derbys DE7 5DA
Tel/Fax: (0115) 932 0643

VESTRY PRAYERS

1. Lord,
What a tremendous promise.
Where two or more are gathered together in
Your Name; You are in the midst.
This is wonderfully reassuring.
Bless Your servant and the message.
Amen.

2. Heavenly Father,
Put Your hand upon our speaker this morning
(evening).
Give them a powerful message,
a clear voice,
and an enthusiastic hearing.
Amen.

3. Lord Jesus,
We need Thee; every hour we need Thee.
None more pressing than now.
May Your Word be proclaimed powerfully.
May Your servant be steadfast and sure.
Let the congregation be filled with Your Spirit.
Amen.

4. Lord,
Bind us together;
the Word, the speaker and the congregation.
We need You in our hearts and minds.
Take this service in praise to You.
Amen.

5. Lord,
As we stand before You,
may we feel Your presence.
Inspire us in our service today.
Give Your messenger a warmth of heart.
Touch souls here this morning/evening.
May Your Spirit be alive to us and within us.
Amen.

6. Father,
We rejoice that we belong to Your family.
Jesus is the head of the Church and leads us on.
May we follow in His footsteps.
May we walk in His love.
Amen.

7. Lord,
With our hearts may we love.
With our hands may we work.
With our voices may we praise.
Hearts, hands, and voices -
What a trio of strength.
Be with us Lord Jesus as we meet in Your name.
Amen.

Suitable for a Flower Festival Service

8. Flowers fill our Church
with shade, variety and colour.
People fill our seats
with shade, variety and colour.
May the flowers teach us a lesson
as they stand side by side.
Bless our service today, Lord.
Amen.

Suitable for a 'Musical' Occasion

9. Dear God,
May song and music bless our service.
We thank You for voices and instruments.
Let all they do together enhance our worship.
Give our preacher inspiration and confidence.
Amen.

Harvest

10. Lord,
What a wonderful time of year, the harvest.
What a variety of produce seen,
the crop.
What a Service of Thankfulness today,
the congregation.
Bring us all together in worship. Amen.

Family or All Age Worship

11. Father,
The children are with us today.
Your Church delights in them.
Bless all ages in our worship;
may we all thrill to Your presence.
A little child shall lead them.
Bless our speaker and those who lead our worship.
Amen.

12. Side by side we pray Lord;
knowing that You are with us.
May Your blessings flow today;
may Your words find fertile ground;
may works done in Your Name expand.
Be amongst us ~~and with us~~.
Bless the message and the messenger.
Amen.

13. Father,
May Your love flow like a river.
Give us an inspired message by and through our speaker today; give Your servant Your power.
May we rejoice in Your Spirit.
Let us know that it has been great to be in the House of our God.
Amen.

14. Jesus we feel You very close.
Speak to us now at the beginning of this service.
May our singing enhance the worship;
let our prayers lead us to action.
May Your Spirit work amongst us.
Amen.

15. We stand before You now Lord.
We wait and listen; then proceed.
Be with our Fellowship this morning/evening
Bless us.
Comfort us.
Strengthen us.
Give our speaker a warmth of heart,
a clear vision,
and a strong message.
Amen.

16. We meet in Your Name Lord.
We rejoice in Your Word.
We worship in Your Spirit.
We labour in Your service.
Stand amongst us now.
Strengthen us, give our speaker inspiration;
lead our rejoicing.
Amen.

17. Lord,
Be our friend.
Be our guide.
Be our leader.
We meet in Your Name,
and know that You are with us, Lord.
Accept what we do in praise to You as Your servant leads us in worship this morning/evening.
Amen.

18. Let your Word reach fertile ground.
May it grow and multiply.
May our Church here be strengthened.
May we go forward in Your Name.
May You lead us into new areas.
Put Your arms around our speaker; may their message be inspiring.
Amen.

19. Enter into all hearts gathered here.
Let the Spirit create harmony and love.
May Your message reach everyone.
Thank You for our speaker;
Thank You for the message they bring.
Bless Your servant and grant them grace divine.
Amen.

20. Father,
May Your Word be inspiring;
May our singing be enthusiastic;
May the message be comforting;
May your servant be strengthened.
Amen.

21. As we lead worship this morning/evening,
Lord be with us.
As we rejoice in Your Name,
Lord be with us.
As we now bow in prayer,
Lord be with us.
As we enter Your House,
Lord be with us.
Amen.

22. Kneeling before You now,
We feel You very near.
Put Your arms around us;
We feel You very near.
Speak to us as we listen;
We feel You very near.
Bless our preacher and inspire him/her.
Amen.

23. At the Name of Jesus,
all shall bow their head.
Enter our hearts Lord;
let us feel You near.
Bless the message;
bless the messenger.
Amen.

24. We call on Your Name Lord.
Be with us, we pray.
Give us Your Holy Spirit.
Cover us in joy.
May Your Word be powerful.
Let the one who leads worship inspire us.
Amen.

25. We marvel at Your creation, Lord.
We marvel that You are mindful of us.
We marvel that You move amongst us.
Bless our service; bless the message.
Bless our congregation; bless Your messenger.
Amen.

Spring

26. It's a sign of Spring, Lord;
a new and exciting season.
New flowers, new plants, new birds, new life.
Bring new life into Your Church.
Bring new life into our hearts.
Bring new life into our work for You.
Be with us Father we pray.
Amen.

27. Let Your love shine in our hearts;
let Your Spirit work amongst us.
May our Church grow in faith and works;
may we listen to Your Word this
morning/evening.
Amen.

28. Every word can come alive when it's written or
read.
May we take Your Word to our hearts
in this time of worship.
May it come alive in our hearts
and take us on to great things.
Amen.

29. Father we stand before You,
in wonder, love and grace.
May we slip our hands into Yours,
knowing that You are with us.
May we give our hearts to You,
asking to be used in Your service.
Be with us we pray this day.
Amen.

30. Silence is golden.
Being still brings us nearer to You.
Quieten our mind.
Widen our thoughts.
Strengthen our faith
use our love in Your name.
Amen.

BENEDICTIONS

1. May we rest in Your peace.
   May we relax in Your love.
   May we rejoice in Your Spirit.
   Go with us now, we pray.
   Amen.

2. Lead the way Lord,
   we will follow
   Be by our side,
   and hand in hand.
   Catch us when we fall,
   hold us if we slip,
   Strengthen us when we falter.
   Amen.

3. Strengthen our faith Lord;
   let it show in works.
   Cultivate our hope Lord;
   let us show it in initiative.
   Widen our love Lord,
   let us show it in friendship.
   Amen.

4. Father,
   May the Good News ring out;
   May the Gospel inspire us;
   May Your teachings make us grow;
   May the Scriptures be our strength.
   Amen.

5. North, South, East, West
   Let the Good News be proclaimed;
   In our towns, cities and villages.
   May we be the inspired messengers.
   Amen.

6. May we go in peace, Lord;
   bringing harmony and happiness.
   May we go in love, Lord,
   taking Your message and Name forward.
   Amen.

7. Forth in Thy Name we go;
Whether we are at work or play,
place the mantle of Your love on us.
Let us proclaim far and wide,
the Name of our Saviour,
and that Jesus is Lord.
Amen.

8. We arise with a Blessing in our hearts.
Let us go forward full of joy;
let us proclaim the Good News
to whoever needs Your Word.
Give us confidence, strength and ability.
In Jesus' Name.
Amen.

9. How the wonderful News spreads;
What a joy to have been present today.
Let this feeling stay with us;
Let the words and sounds remain.
What talents You have given us Lord!
Amen.

10. Trust and obey –
what great words by the hymn writer.
May today's message go forward into tomorrow.
Let us trust the words of Scripture;
Let us obey the words of command.
Bless each and everyone, Lord.
Amen.

11. What a friend we have in Jesus;
Let us ask the Lord to walk by our side.
Hand in hand let us face the world together.
There is no stronger bond.
There is no firmer comrade.
Go with us on our way.
Amen.

12. Evening shadows fill the sky;
Another day is coming to an end.
We thank You Lord for what has gone;
We rejoice in what is to be.
Let us put our hand into Yours,
Knowing that You go with us always.
Amen.

13. An inspiring service!
Devotional prayers; meaningful singing; expressive readings.
May our hearts feel strangely warmed with Your love,
Accept our praise tonight.
Amen.

14. Another day; another week; another month.
Time waits for no man.
We are in Your world Father.
Let us obey your call.
Amen.

15. What a team we make;
Working together brings success.
Take our works in praise;
Strengthen our faith in worship.
Go with us on our way;
Be by our side now and always.
Amen.

16. We have looked;
We have listened.
We have worshipped
We now feel strong in faith.
May we take our talents
and spread the Good News of Jesus.
Amen.

17. Take our lives and let them be used
in total service to You Lord.
May we never be afraid to venture forth
in Your Name.
Together we can move mountains.
Amen.

18. This is a happy day;
Our wrongs have been taken away.
Forth in Your Name we venture, Lord.
Guide us,
lift us,
strengthen us.
Your power will see us through.
Amen.

19. Take our lives,
Take our moments,
Take our days,
Take our love.
All we have belongs to You Lord;
All our talents have been given to us;
Let us use them in Your service.
Amen.

20. Let the power of God be with us;
Let the love of the Lord Jesus bless us;
Let the Spirit direct and rule our hearts.
In Your great Name we rejoice.
Go with us now and every day.
Amen.

21. Go with us to our homes.
Venture forth with us to our families.
Be by our side as we meet friends.
You are the great Comforter and Guide.
Amen.

22. May we be as the pebble cast into the water;
May we be as the ripples expanding outward;
May we reach for new opportunities
to do Your work and service.
Amen.

23. There's a sparkle in our eyes;
There's a smile upon our faces.
Our hearts are strangely warmed;
Our step is strong and lively.
We walk with the Lord;
We hope all will see this.
Thank You for the joy You bring us.
Amen.

24. At the end of the day
Let us just kneel and pray.
Take us into Your world.
Give us love in our hearts;
Strength in our works;
Renewal in our faith.
Amen.

25. Let us dare to be a Daniel;
Let us proclaim our faith anew.
Let us stand up for what is true;
Let us go forth in Your Name.
Amen.

26. The letters of NEWS
Give us North, East, West and South;
All four corners of our world.
Let us go forth and proclaim;
Let us take Your Word afar;
Let us make people aware of the Gospel.
In Jesus' Name
Amen.

27. Your love is like a river:
may it flow.
Our faith is like the wind:
let it be strong.
Hope is like the sun:
shining and getting brighter.
Faith, hope, and love:
all are Your gifts Father.
Amen.

28. The Word became flesh and dwelt amongst us.
Jesus is alive and with us.
May He enter each heart;
May our faith be enhanced;
May His love be our strength.
Amen.

29. Let us arise and go forth.
Let us go in the Name of
The Father, the Son and the Holy Spirit.
Our great values are in the Trinity.
Let us take them into the workplace,
The office, the school, the home.
Be with us evermore and bless us.
Amen.

30. We are so happy,
that You are mindful of us.
We rejoice that worship
has warmed our hearts.
We know that You have been in our midst.
Let us go forth in Your great name.
Let us proclaim the Gospel to all.
Let your church grow in this area.
Amen.

GRACES

1. A piece of cake
   For you to take,
   Is on the table now.

   A cup of tea
   For you and me
   We can't refuse – how!

   In thoughtful mood,
   It's thanks for food,
   As our heads we bow.
   Amen.

2. We thank You that we meet together.
   We thank You for afternoon tea.
   We thank You for simple delights.
   Accept our grace said before You now.
   It is right and good to be thankful.
   Father, hear our prayer.
   Amen.

3. For this opulent occasion,
These memorable moments,
The fabulous food,
And cordial company,
With words and hearts
We thank You now Father.
Amen.

4. Let's pause awhile to give our praise,
For fellowship together on special days.
We've happy thoughts of come what may,
Seeing this table full of rich array.
It seems so sure we're to be well fed,
Accept this grace for a super spread.
Amen.

5. Grace is now upon our lips
As we sit down to eat.
Cooking, smelling, very well
Done to a turn our meat.
Thank You Lord for it all.
The salad, rolls and bread.
We promise to enjoy it now
So let's lift up our head.
Amen.

6. Burgers, sausages, chops, are cooking.
Now we say our grace:
Thank You Lord for a super time,
For food and drinks together.
Thank You Lord for a wonderful evening
Fun, refreshment and friends.
Amen.

Breakfast

7. Another day; another start.
We have before us a super breakfast, Lord.
What a wonderful way to begin a new morning.
Thank You for all we see on our table.
May we depart from this meal satisfied
And ready for what is to come.
Amen.

8. For the usual breakfast mix;
Fruit juice, flakes or weetabix.
We thank You now whilst bowing our head
And wait for bacon and fried bread.
Amen.

9. *A Snack*

Thank You Lord for our daily break,
Tea, coffee, biscuits or cake.
A few minutes off is all that's required,
To make us fit again and not too tired.
Amen.

10. *A Break*

A few minutes make for this welcome break.
We wait, our plates are bare
With this prayer: thanks for the fare,
All seems right, so let's bite.
A welcome rest; let's do our best.
We'll not shirk; now to work.
Amen.

11. Lord, thank You for our friends at work.
Thank You for our jobs.
Thank You for giving us skills and abilities.
We thank You now Lord for a break;
A few minutes to get back our strength,
Thank You for the refreshment provided.
Amen.

12. *A Buffet*

It's time for the buffet
Something to bite.
This takes us on into the night.
Little and often is the need.
Accept our thanks,
For all the feed.
Amen.

13. *For an Annual Dinner/Dance etc*

As annually we enjoy this Ball.
Accept our praise for table wealth,
Given to us to sustain our health.
So may the compliments be many
So all can say – 'worth every penny!'
Amen.

14. Heads bowed – A request to all;
Back to basics is the call.
Grace to start, standards set.
Thank You Lord for the food we get.
All give You praise for table fare.
Let's sit down and take our share.
Amen.

15. *Fish and Chip Supper*

We have to say as we pray this grace,
Thank You for a tasty dish;
Fish, chips and peas before us now.
We are so grateful for this plateful.
Amen.

16. *Bangers and Mash Supper*

The bangers are great,
The mash so white.
Thank You Dear Lord,
For a real great night.
Amen.

17. *A Church Dinner*

Lord, on this occasion we feel good.
The night before us, so we should.
Accept this grace, short though it be,
For things to come and what we see.
Our thanks for fellowship, fun and food,
this Church event puts us in good mood.
Resplendent now in bow and gown
Let's take our chair and all sit down.
Amen.

18. Grace is now part of the plan
For the gifts you've given to man.
Accept our thanks for all the courses,
The wonderful variety and super sauces.
Now in anticipation of our food
We sit together in party mood.
Amen.

19. Thanks now spoken
Are the token
For the feed,
Grace indeed.
Soup in a bowl,
Crusty roll.
Sweet in a dish,
What a wish.
Your selection,
To perfection.
Wonderful.
Amen.

20. *A Bar Meal*

How happy we are
Gathered round the bar
With our chosen meal now coming.
We've finished the talk
And with knife and fork
say, "Thank You Lord, it's ready!"
With praise from our heart
We're eager to start.
Ready to eat what You give us.
Amen.

21. Jacket potatoes with delicious filling
Are on the menu, what a billing.
For such a meal now,
and for all Your care.
Accept our grace for this fine fare
Amen.

22. *A break on a ramble*

Time to gaze around and stare
From rambling in the open air.
A quiet sit down, a timely break,
A welcome rest for all our sake.
Our grace to say, so let it be
Thank You Dear Lord for a cup of tea.
Amen.

23. It's fruit and veg from the ground
Which now fill the tables around.
These foods in their dishes,
Will now satisfy our wishes.
For this time out of real pleasure
Accept our grace in sincerest measure.
Amen.

24. Father ,
Accept our thanks for:
The splendour of the occasion,
The warmth of the fellowship,
The waiting, anticipating appetite,
The loaded tables of delight,
The evening in front of us.
This is our grace now said.
Amen.

25. *A Takeaway Meal*
For all the things we have with chips,
We give You praise now with our lips.
A meal so simple is on the table today
Delivered so quickly from a takeaway.
Accept our grace with thanks, dear Lord
For giving us part of nature's reward.
Amen.

26. Let's not take more than we need
To satisfy our daily need.
Remembering to get up wanting more,
Go from the table, through the door.
Accept our grace for abundant love,
And hear our prayers now, Lord above.
Amen.

27. *A Buffet Lunch*
A light lunch is on the table now.
We close our eyes and humbly bow.
A finger buffet, with drinks in place,
No better reason to say our grace.
So thank You Lord, for a mid-day rest
And giving us all what is the best.
Amen.

28. *A Chairman's Grace*
It is one of those red letter days
So let us bow our heads in praise.
A night out, now top of the bill
The tables full to give us all our fill.
What a lovely evening it's going to be
As in anticipation we wait and see.
It's now my year here in the Chair
So may I do it all with style and flair.
Amen.

29. *A Reunion*

How good it is to keep this date,
To look around and see a mate.
Time has brought so much change
Since last we were together.
So let us make the most of this time now
As for our grace we humbly bow.
Thank You Lord for opportunities past,
We trust and hope our friendships last.
Amen.

30. When gazing at our table of fare
It makes us gasp and bow in prayer.
There's so much food to eat indeed,
but keep us mindful of those in need.
Accept our grace and hear our cry
As we come before Your throne on high.
Amen.